W9-CTY-752

The Beauty Wars

The Beauty Wars

Carol Conroy

W·W·Norton & Company

New York   London

P   O   E   M   S

Grateful acknowledgment is made to The Agni Review *in which "The Woman Who Held Waterfalls" and "The Deer Man" first appeared.*

Printed in the United States of America.

The text of this book is composed in 10.5/13 Garamond No.3 (8 pt. master), with the display set in ITC Garamond Bold Condensed.

Composition and manufacturing by The Maple-Vail Book Manufacturing Group.

Book and ornament design by Margaret M. Wagner.

First Edition

Library of Congress Cataloging-in-Publication Data
Conroy, Carol.
The beauty wars / Carol Conroy.
p.   cm.
I. Title.
PS3553.O519B4   1991
811'.54—dc20   *90–38622*

ISBN 0–393–02920–4

W. W. Norton & Company, Inc., 500 Fifth Avenue, New York, N.Y. 10110
W. W. Norton & Company, Ltd., 10 Coptic Street, London WC1A 1PU
1 2 3 4 5 6 7 8 9 0

In memory of my mother,
Margaret Peek Conroy Egan

For my father, Colonel Donald Conroy, USMC (Ret.)
For my sister, Kathleen Harvey
For Naoko Nakamura

Contents

Therefore, as One returned, I feel
Odd secrets of the line to tell!
Some Sailor, skirting foreign shores—
Some pale Reporter, from the awful doors
Before the Seal!

—EMILY DICKINSON

Send your second soul beyond the mountains, beyond time.
Tell me what you saw, I will wait.

—CZESLAW MILOSZ

I

Bloodlines and Flight

Children of Gullah

It's time I talked about the boiling South.
We bought *people*. We sold *people*.

Swift mansions, beating the air:
the raped girl, the hanged man.
My birdsong and my white South.

I put my finger on a map.

Its crinkled markings shame the family tree.
I am the grandchild of hate,
crosses burning, inside me.

The brown arm of a continent torn off.

Filled, the drums of salt, with human limbs.
Where to begin? Africa gripped.
They natured a myth,
first death in the hold.

O conjureman, go on with us.

They must have known the dark was brokenhearted,
when slave boats ploughed a cracker surf,
and cried her magic blood in guilty lots.

O conjureman, fly off, fly off.

They must have known an Angelus of hills
rode wondrous down, when Mansweat sang in cotton rows,
each vertebra a pair of 'Bama mules,
each spirit-chord a tune of banjo ice.

In the great raised country of the trees,
the conjureman be flying home.

How many bullsnakes whipped cyclonic stars,
out of his hissing, sideways cape?
Did he ask hell for sleet tonight?

The goriot has rainbowed up.

Sundial to cattle and infinite sheep,
his canny hoof chinked dew;
Black Angus begat a bawling moon,
hidebound and cut.

In the book of days, write down it shone.

Biography of rivers flowing North:
people hungry, people cold.
The Judgment freed the tremolo
trapped in the wood.

Dark-throated birds changed back to men.

Ghost-girl Combs at Ribbon Creek

1

There is a monument in the District of Columbia
where spun-rain delicately crystals
voweled foxholes.
The vortex of an angle, a wronged
angle, looms and depresses.
The uncanny

parade of their flesh
salutes spattered families into stone.
The wall darkly wails:
it *names*.
Black fire on white fire.
I speak here of runes.

I speak here of fathers', sons',
brothers', friends', lifers', grunts', and sexy
kids dead as tombs.
The first boy I kiss on Ribaut Road
at a spin-the-bottle party, my lips almost perish on lips.
Others because he died.

I hold here the men we touched,
who touched us
in passionate positions,

not knowing
the last embrace was the last;
not knowing the exact

itinerary of copters, spookies, battalions, blood—scream
after bathy scream—the infinite shock—routinely
ziplocked in bags.
This is the wall
they built
from a grazing loyal alphabet

of mortared bones
we shall never
unspell.
Once upon a wall
I rub a name.
But not again.

2

Finally,
the commandant of Nightmares
recruits my maple hair;
unspools my triple-braid and sweeps the floor.

Tonight I comb at Ribbon Creek.
If lost,

look for a broom of human hair.
If found,
out of the throats of threshing boys
I shall pass and review
my life; their death.
Stunned

in a trance on the fraught shores
Tripoli,
there was a girl
with a sabered mouth, blasted and drilled
in masculine beauty.
I knew her when.

The Parris Island calisthenic band!
the sit-up brass! the drum-roll grub! the winded men!
Discipline and ecstasy: the taste
of sweat, shyly,
stirring my mouth, 0600 the dawn,
where I dance alone, boldly, the obstacle course.

Medals of boys—
in mullioned windows; across spit-polished aisles,

PX lieutenants; in Quonset hut doorframes,
buck privates and gun butts; quick-time
fatigues and rifle
range fire;

in off-duty library stacks,
unfurled MPs; sunglassed sentries frisking the gate;
lamp-eyed arrivals; in sheepish barbershop
chairs, wispy curl-pillows;
they were everywhere,
gleaming.

3

Death is working,
sir, an April moonless link.
Old Nightmare, the marshes, the tidal-swift
Ribbon, mudbank to the chill,
58°,
murky stream rising.

On the eighth day of zeal, Staff
Sergeant McKeon, pulled muscle throbbing,
a broomstick his crutch, hobbles into the barracks.

74 boots
fall out in 2 minutes.
The long line of geography

is dissecting the boondocks.
Soldiers
in country! the column rakes treacherously
into the slippage, the marching
boots into the foreign mudcarpet siege
wall high and rising.

Death is dragging,
sir, a tidal-swift chain.
Leathernecks
who serve—6 who drowned—"Semper Fidelis."
Bobbing upstream,
ribbons and ribbons and ribbons of snakes.

1956:
the United States Military Tribunal:
the Corps on trial:
"that it is the mission of this command to produce Marines."
I do not sing a martial art.
I *weep*

casualties and veterans.
Men like McKeon—men like my father.
Present arms and report:
Rain!
the aviator's daughter,
a jet of velvet water.

4

I cut my hair at Ribbon Creek.
I cut my hair where boys sank down.

M.I.A. / P.O.W.

And Time the Soldier
in the greenthroat of the river
in the shako of the current
sobs going and seems gone;
And Time the Agent
in the tigerpits of flash
in the sorties of the jungle
blows orange hair and coughs.

The Fighter Pilot

The stars are colder
in my father's dream. At thirty thousand feet
black sheep bawl and constant shepherds, less the wind,
stand by for pilots. The Dipper points.
The war is over and the conflict has begun.

The stars are brighter
in my father's dream. The instrument panel fades.
Close as wheels the carrier till the *Sicily,* add the sea-
roll, shags away. The gas is down and he is not.
Say hey Pacific.

The stars are thicker
in my father's dream. So! Now chaos buckles
Orion's belt and snaps Saigon.
The man who loved Aviation
retires to ride the beautiful, dark engines in his sleep.

The Great Santini's Wild, Sleek Children

Skyhawk, Dauntless, Corsair, Avenger, Hellcat, Panther, and *Pilot Dawn.*

Tears for Roberto Clemente

1

The only time my father weeps
is the middle of the night a plane goes down:
Roberto Clemente is dead.

Is it you, my fatherland, I see
cry those uphill
steely tears ruffling the neck-
feathers of a flyaway
girl—*I come to hold?*

Pilots and athletes are genies of speed,
but this gravity called love happens on earth.

2

And I wonder
really, why I wondered
so little, when rudimentary stairrot
rails my blood away
from you, who sits axe-still,
frozen, while I shine down

the steps again, as bright as any
runway in the pure
undershirting of the father.

3

Deep from the salt-
hum of dream traffic patterns, I look
for the jug-earred water, but divine instead
grief. Now
the crash landing of your kitchen
talk helpless to help
tender to rant
   the ballplayer
     coal-in-his-mouth
   in a plane-storming-kingdom
     who shouted in sooty
   leatherglove Spanish
     the untranslatable:
       the error of sky.

And I can remember
wings in the room, and those lost blackbird
tears, sliding
cleat

points of pity
whispering with you:
"sweet Roberto Clemente, my boyo, my boy."

4

Forgive me in summer, Roberto Clemente,
who did not feel then, aberration
of orelight, nor the eclipse;
and tell me, my boyo, how fares the Slugger
in the furnace of heroes?

5

I pitch it back,
my heaven of fathers, that stable
of legends, where nightmares drink stars,
and daughters go thirsty
with midnight birds
bathing in sandlots.

Give me the horselaugh
from a herd of wild players.
Fetch me matching iron shoes
to stamp a rust river.

All the ruined wings, the night-
tears for Roberto, and my father
broken—I will tag up!
and I will speak well of.

The Craft of Dying

in memory of Colm Walsh

Let Irish kings prepare a twilight race
to blind a dazzled mirror, shot with sea.
Tonight majestic stars become your face.

Grief is a homesick ballad, and no place
for clouds of knowing what a cloud can see.
Let Irish kings prepare a twilight race.

Who cuts the moon? Who hems a scudding lace?
Great mother night adores a lampblack bee.
Tonight majestic stars become your face.

Pale horses and horizon are erased:
hold tight, my love, in gripping memory.
Let Irish kings prepare a twilight race,

where laughing reivers lead a hellish chase.
But lock the sky, and tumble all the keys.
Tonight majestic stars become your face.

Like harebells blown, a wilder form of grace;
the newly dead are beautiful, and free.
Let Irish kings prepare a twilight race.
Tonight majestic stars become your face.

Starfish

A solemn child stood near an ocean,
applauding the reckless
drama,
and a red mask rose slowly on that curtain,
and a gold mask
sank
inside her deeper, *why*
the sickle moon
swung
the wild sun
lit
a magic pier on stilts.
Brave Players
on a boundless horizon
strutting through the body of a girl,
who bowed, who disappeared,
like slimming shadows
into the legend
of water,
the first morning I hold a star beneath a wave,
and know it dark against my waist,
secret I keep.

The Southern Cross

"Aurum nostrum non est aurum vulgum"

The boys of Howard Beach may never pound
coalsack points into a sacred token.
Feeding a tiny god-mouth underground,

I reconstruct a tooth, mica-broken.
Mystery is this temple crowd at night.
I have seen freedom magnify a cheek;

over a bowl of slag one head grew light.
I have seen engines after furied leaks.
Marvelous ratchet whose spark outflung

the concrete ghetto in a rounding car!
Let me be cable croaking the unsung—
to take a human hand and take it far.

In starry sheets a thorn has rusted down:
the children of the rood fly underground.

I I

Reconstruction

*for Nancye Faulkner Belding, Rose Jensen,
and Bonnie Jetty*

The Strength of Wounds

Far back in my eyes is this childhood
where Round Look trances an ear.

And I in the tall corn listen;
bride of the cosmic plot.

The sky-groat millers its cake:
nine metal planets of night.

Everywhere covers the grass,
but the soul walks naked, staring.

When I face the folded wolf,
my breathing stops.

The executioner lifts his blade;
loose robe flapping.

The knife is printed—
not ink, but my book leaks redly.

Corpse, my pond-lids grow heavy:
I hide in the future.

Some black and fertile place
receives these bones.

Thonged in a glitten mass,
blossoms transmember the trees.

My sister, the wind,
makes a tear.

It's a slain girl alive in the bog.
Beauty matted with songs.

The Woman Who Held Waterfalls

There is no photograph but memory
to save what happens at Great Falls,
the last moment I am a child
like other children.

My mother rinsing tea leaves in the sink
reads the future; snaps the beans.
My father snores B-52's;
he wakes up, landing.

Just a family picnic in late July
in the heat of a skittish month,
when helping hands cartwheel over
before adventure.

The house of summer has a fire door.
It is not solid, ladybug.
A whiffle ball puffs through the swings;
the wind in spaces.

I pay the telescope my shining change:
first the red sock and then the white:
a carousel breaks out and rears
a flight of horses.

O focus on a string of tawny shapes!
a game of dare across bright rock—
the lion-colored boy who slips
the thunderous falls.

The water rises, and the water parts.
I move in sound waves not myself
but the breath of a spilling boy
suddenly roaring.

There is no rescue except flesh and blood.
I grant the air its pride of place;
parachute silk I pulled that boy
inside my faithful body.

A Field Guide to Open Caskets

The casket buckled
my smaller
shoe,
the day my grandfather disappeared
behind a stone wall with a plaque.
I carried the flower of his name,
Jack-
in-the-pulpit
into the bedrock mausoleum.
Since not a single glow-worm burnished
that scrolled earth of engraving,
I apprenticed mulching.

From lap to kiss
of apple snuff
I heard the vanguard
in the parlor
bawl "Carol Ann
was on his lips—
the poor burr dying."

The horsehair sofa
bristled up and I
clutched fast the stem
of him as tart and
clucking country gentles
tried to read the palm
I could not open.

They wailed; they
parsed a windy hilltop sermon:
"Barefoot he maunders.
He totes a pinecone branch for puny chirl'ren."

One child ran up!
up the creaky spine of the house
to the mice room
he never entered.

The dust was mine.
But the trunk in the attic
belonged to my mother's mother's mother;
and it was made of cedar
to keep secrets' Ella Donna,
who clogged a mash of shadows in boot
moon Alabam.

Tenderly,
I struck the lid,
and lifting bride taws laceabilia,
I pulled all white
things darkly over.

When the box was shut
I knew myself

the way a nest
its own dried leafiness
and rudecast twigs
knows any bird.

Behind a key of light
I spied a web
—a snow egg—
colder than a chink of whistle-wood.

And when the spider danced:
And when the dead sang up the stairs:
And when a bat commenced to flap a moving picture
    across a knotty board—I like to died.

I held my body
to my body
and felt the house
dig in its corners
as I popped
Jack-
in-the-box
under starlings' bill-dark roof.

Inside the chest
of my mother's mother's mother, once

I breathed that dank ferocious lavender—potent memory.
I grew a flower
to name *my* name.

I said goodbye,
grandfather love—
on a Appalachian quilt I shall tat you
and in a crib of purple shadows
I shall featherstitch a full
county of moths,
and a civil township of worms for your own fine business.

Journey to the Underworld

I *loved* him.
I was the pagan
who found him black and rubbed
him pewter.
Night into space, I waxed a sacred path, dorsal and heft,
and watered him,
keening.
Lord of the krill!
Huge spouter hole blow!

I was a prophet on a beached whale's back.

The mountain died.
Snorting plough of waves, Leviathan
broke.

The maw entombed and echoed me.

I did not know my address in the skald-light;
or how I spiderized a mucus web across a chasm;
or how I caught a fish with hideout teeth
    like bayonets;
or how I came to swing the whitenesses of bones the size of trees
    and mowed them down;
or how I tore an oozing acre from a field, and shrunk
    a mammal's face the other side of nature.

Why should these wild palms distress me? A certain catapulting
    season, beyond the breakers . . .

Cathedral of the sea,
what starry roof could hove such bottom-
slabbed beauty, God's
humped tear,
without funeral rites and cups of fire as shaken coral bells
have clapped and flumed ashore?

What floating Stonehenge? What storied torch?
he beached he died he spirited the ground he flattened.

The Great Depression

I dreamt my troubles were riches.
Expensively I dressed in sorghum.
Pacing the back forty,
I grew hemp bast
in my beard
to hang a body
dearly.
I kicked at the stars—
(dangle dangle a pig goddess tree).
Little debts plucked:
a volley of crows
burst out of me
music.
And I cawed and wondered in the bight.
And I blinked in the crater of pale mules.
And I snapped
tingling
back.

Once I was a straw man on a limb;
scratched I was, but solvent!
Sure filled my cheeks with acorns.
Sure waved a fortune at the bank.

Do Lord reckon the mortgage my ass.

The Boatman of Light

1

Darkness:
a man walking by a river,
hooded and pensive, on the land.
The river is chanting darkly to a man.
A nameless rider points downstream,
on the tidewhip, past the town.
Darker: a man, a body of water,
and a corpse.
And for what purpose?

2

And the corpse keeps coming,
and it moves inside us,
and despair is the dead weight
floating into the eyes . . .

3

Each life drifting down the brackish current
once held a passion flower between its teeth,
like a bit that clamps the spirit or helps
to take the sandbar and keep straining
toward a morgue where temperatures drop off
and nothing remains but initiation.
Death: she be the slow barge chuffing
this way—only one-among-so-many
goes out to meet her,
to reclaim our cargo.

4

Take comfort, Monet is on the river
the morning a torn unmuscled iris redeems a race.
Only the dead come to kiss the wet mouths of flowers.
        This is greatness;
not the brutal assault on fragrance,
but the surface watermark of all our gliding prayers.
            Imagine,
on pads like petals
frogs spawned out of princely sea-green wits
trust the day they are born to sustain them.

Flitting on the splayed fingers
of an elemental glove
a feed of insects
hears the amphibian jaw
snap around them
much too late.
Monet is present.
His ears buzz and his eyes
try to see what he has seen.

5

He waited.
The man who carried light
inside his belly
waited for a midwife
with a candle dripping fire.
He grew.
But each time he reached
for color he made
absence of it.
A shirtless man
whistled
the wind.
His water broke.
So he pissed in the grass

of the gypsies.
Only the hounds
adored the birthheat in the night,
deep in their dream of the pack,
brattling the miles
beside him.

6

Have courage;
carry it with you as you go.
Fill your pockets with useful items:
paints and brushes and quick-spied monies
dropped on the splendiferous elm boulevard
by the purse-lipped estate dweller; be sure
to select the ripest cheese; also bring a pocketknife
with a blade that folds in and away from injury.

7

How obviously the macabre end
shores around the soul

after an ardent cathedral priest dims the bells
and pulls himself through the implicating weeds
like a rope vibrating sacramental music
      where river rushes
      spills
      flinting forth
      vision
      far beyond the flowerfalls of reason.

8

Let the body purify itself,
and do not despair for the flower.
Kiss the light around the object.
Monet is on the river.
The Boatman of Light will never leave,
not in your lifetime, and you cannot drown,
you cannot even sink beneath
the murky waters of error
if you scream
and let yourself rip open.
Bear down.

III

Grandmother Sampler

for Stanny

Empress of Games

1

I have an enormous wish, to praise dark-calling-units.
How great is January—the gate of glow.

2

Chenille bedspreads vaulting red rope lines,
washer February, a-leaping year.

3

You, mill brides and sun-mooing cities!
In riddle March I solve a hill.

4

Impatience, wait;
April-spawn makes lace-wing May.

5

June tags July—
two magicals touch all mortal joy.

6

O fire, by inlet, burning logs,
August scuttles, barrelhot.

7

September's nature wildly sniffs
pelt of loam, egg, and ur.

8

I see where stars go when they sleep:
October starlings move the sky.

9

This is the meadow where girls get lost,
in a dawn of blood, menstrual.

10

These are the souls of months that come for women
my first November, ever.

11

The death of great December drops the curtain
to carry snowflakes to a revel.

12

Radiance drags that ancient wheel.
How great is Time—rough, smooth; spindle, turn.

13

An Empress sang humors on my head;
the days are spinning tops that whirl in season.

Empress of Prayers

for Patricia Hampl

1

I have a tremendous need, to bless prime-burning-functions.
How vast is Air—the hinge of Om.

2

Adventure sounds us, it stretches.
What is grace but nerve in tune with living tissue?

3

To sally forth through mundane fields,
and then return—slipper moist—this is holy.

4

The world reflects the universe;
the word reflects the soul.

5

In the garden, the little garden, of mystic points,
a stem of sunlight holds the sky.

6

The power of absence also keeps,
like a spaceship in a bottle, shaking stars.

7

Transubstantiation—
testimony across the Milky Way.

8

These are the eyelids of faith-in-vision:
I am chosen O Transparent chosen.

9

Religion begins in the red house of the body,
when the dance of selves illuminates the holy heart.

10

Jerusalem, dream—
the flesh trembles: the soul unwinds.

11

Eternity snaps the twig.
Each whorled grain documents existence.

12

Creatrix on the mount!
How vast is Space—cosmos, psyche; Moon-tree, host.

13

An Empress lit torches in my mouth;
brightness be my manger and my straw.

Empress of Colors

1

I have a seamless wish, to chart bright-wheeling-signs.
How wild is Magic—a pride of moons.

2

Our Lady of Rainy Springs
stained glass Anima.

3

Baskets of Europe, gentian, violet;
O sway and celebrate the windmill's azure wife.

4

Yet what is exultation but some highland roar—
skirling trees in that cat-yellow wind.

5

Listen! whippoorwill green:
bird to willow.

6

Indestructible orange,
I touch your newborn cheek, river-fruit.

7

Blackjetted bees, swift as fire,
chase the mad red queen.

8

At sea-bruise tide,
a purple sage approaches foam.

9

Passion delights a crystal fork,
where lightning clarity chuckles like thunder.

10

Parachute,
I am falling down the faint roof of blue love-in-a-mist.

11

Love never loved you enough?
Who put that goldmaking hole in your chest.

12

You, raucous laughter and jar-bearing tears!
How wild is Birth—water, blood; innocence, age.

13

An Empress dragged rainbows from my eyes.
Liquid bridge, I see a stream, these ecstatic new trains.

Empress of Forms

1

I have a sleepless plan, to free crane-pooling-signatures.
How deep is Grief—a beak of tears.

2

Nothing is more blithe than baby feet
born flying.

3

Old stagers whistle the grandest tune:
More.

4

To look at the mountain's face,
climb the bonehouse of Creation.

5

Stone soldiers on moon-bleached squares
bronze the silent carnage of every Gothic childhood.

6

An alphabet is a swarming hive,
but a word is royal jelly.

7

On Widow loch a coffin floats over diamond
rings.

8

The power of presence also stirs,
like a blizzard in a glass, clinking ice.

9

Ghost of the Tribal Hand,
I have come to wake the soft powers of remembrance.

10

I place you, mother—unaware—Penelope by the loom,
and wonder if you weave my tomb.

11

Wild flaxseed of the missing field,
may I whisper the jenny-wheel that churns in the sea?

12

Little flowers of the coral reef!
How deep is Death—diver, mask; fever, chill.

13

An Empress rolled my belly East.
Let me fly out the shapes of our passionate lives.

Rising

Evolution of the Woman as Artist

Night and Day

The bloodtie is magical:
you piece me together and saw me in half.

Let this banshee
pass powerfully through me. *Wombgame,*
teach me; press
me to the scrolled pith of papyrus: my heart
is beating inside a fetal
clock.
Anatomy of darkness,
how innocent the guilt of children.

My eyes are galaxies
and terror. I creep to the cellar
how many centuries too late? Under a blotter
sun
I descend. A garlic
bulb gives no
light no
light.

My ears are hornet hives
and sting.
The Vampire echo-chamber shrieks:

"Y'all come back now."
"Y'all come back now."

The nightshade. The pillow.
The goose: down
I mean.

Just silver warlocks,
unconscious, nothing to be accused of,
yet.
They muse at dusk.
A brooding
priest draws out a crusted quill
from his old,
wet side. This is my cue—the Vampire swoon.

Mistletoe Mistletoe
Psyche in hell
my casket is lead
my face is pale.

Brother Hawk!
Sister Owl!
Nothing grows more tired than a
wing.
I dream it.

I open a box
of feathers
flying home.
I find the egg.
I drop it.

You dead.
Me dead.
Ow.

Bring mythic peacocks with their fine excess,
and let the feathers tell flamboyant stories.

Out of the radiant cunt of all dead queens,
out of *Crocus* and *Skull* and *Elephant* and *Castle,*
out of harlot and crone and wife and abbess and maid,
I hear *Anonymous*
knocking.
From the last, red leaf to the menstrual prelude,
from the sibling straitjacket to the rapturous sibyl,
from a mortal sketch to an absolute portrait,
we blaze
out. Syllables of light take our names.

The stage is bare,
This is another world.

Sun and Moon

Dark plumes of genesis and swirling fans of eyes along the Nile,
    where brother and sister bed, dismembering gods.

Nor mouth told.
Nor mealworm feasted.
Nor pyramid inched in the moon.

Relic
and fossil!
The saddest route I shall ever trace is this
one: sister-brother
River limb.

Let this blunt
orange No. 2 pencil
grind exceedingly sharp. *Stylus,*
illuminate me; restore
me to the sums of the Old City: my face
is moving across the cleft
horizon,
day and night,
to draw the seething hieroglyph of Incest from the womb.

Heart's Blood,
in the house of mystic water,
in the straw-gold sac of the dreamers,
in the daring zygote of Gemini spinning and flashing
starfully,
we sailed around the amniotic horn and tumbled
mortal into the light
of rosy death.

There should have been a universe of scissor arms
to cut us premature
apart.

Twin ball of fire,
twin ball of feet,
the alpha-stick scratches each signature
Alone.

Nothing grows more tired than a
curse.
I do it.
I do not harm one hair on a small boy's
head,
but I rend,
and hammer,
and pound the parasitic bond

between this man
and me.

I swallow a thousand years of prehistoric mold.
I hum my shadow through the gate;
I dance
with voices
underground.

In my mother's womb are many natures.

Out of a rubied, gnarled earth of giant redwoods,
out of the heat and violence of volcanic dust,
out of lava and drought and runnel and cinnabar and ice,
I liquid-shoulder forth
a self—
a single ray
of life.
No hand has ever lifted this particular
stone before:
whosoever finds the Navel
cave is fire-
born, diamond-scorched, mineral-graced, and unbetrayably
baptized in gold.

Beyond the pale
house of incest
I meet my great brother-soul
in the scarab
tide, where uncreated bones clutch pens of fire.
Bright, fluent life!
River-sang.

                    An old, old bridge.
                        I walk it.

When You Ask This Riddle . . . *

*I'd as lief pray with Kit Smart as any
man in London.*—BEN JONSON

Genius of the fire-leaping harp,

Let the white, sad iron press my sobbing roots.

Let dragons belch stars.

Let wise men scatter—my soul is homeless and my limbs are cold.

Let Love, the holy boy, take aim.

Let the moon nock my talons.

Bury my bride in a cranberry bog when killing
    spring has fled.

Let oceans break soakingly into wild, airy fragments.

Let the I I am spawn future tablets.

Let a great stone circle dance elephantine suns to a powder
    turbulent with ants.

O jubilating rainbow in the rain!

Let swamp-drop woo pear-seed on myrrh blossom wind.

Let consecrated doves mysteriously chime.

* Antiphon—see answering page.

Answer Hummingbird Smart

put glory on the sun gem and let the sylph go by.

For I am the Messiah of thorns.

For I am spangled topaz, isle of warlight, age-yellow.

*For I am the keelstroke of midnight, bladelike Mary, swimming
through Bethlehem.*

For I am a quivered leaf, shot from a tree.

For I am the Druid owl.

*For I am the roué of petals, ruby-throated, swooning
above roses.*

For I am a sea horse galloping treasures up.

For I am the chain-letter of continents in fingerlake salmon tones.

For I am swift among Lilliputians.

*For I am infant violetears on a waterfall's bib, ecstatically
flung, vermillion.*

For I am the riddle of the small, and my badge is gorget.

For I am the "Mona Birda" in a gallery of diminished masterpieces.

Let the gift of noon comfort the simple.
Let Smoke, son of Zero, burn.

Let mummers walk naked with animal eyes.
Let honey thicken.
Let flesh, king of bones, prime the sweet house of blood.

For I am a hill star gypsy who hasn't any shadow.

*For I am endlust of the Paraclete, clouds of tongues, meaning
flames! flames! flames! including roller, king-
fisher, and accidental hornbill the hornblower.*

For I am pretty Madwing, deeply humming.

For I am bee-sip needles.

For I am red.

The Romantic Fallacy

Hero was a girl.
She killed herself for cold love.
Heroes make mistakes.

The Poet to the Mime

for Chris Cinque

I meet "the lovers" in Atlanta,
in the lost island of a woman's bar.
The Tower is the place they come together.
They are deaf mutes.
They are talking through the air.

I am alone
and I am sad;
it is my birthday.

The deaf mutes blaze with agile poems,
their arms light torches overhead,
four rippling flames of bone
that climb the stairs.
When the wind blows you back,
I touch your arm.
The whisper of one hand
can spur a song.

    I still say your name softly,
    I say *Marie* with dancing hands.
    Lesbian is the word I say too loud—
    volume the fear that breaks
    the surface where you swim
    the anger that such lovely leaps offend.
    My love dissolves in ambergris some days

and leaves a wake of silver scales
to cover with a bright illicit cape.

Marie,
you did not write.
I ask a red-haired mute to tell me why.
The Mime,
does she send messages too,
are fingers frozen in a northern lake,
is this the reason?
I lived there once
and should remember.
I forget myself,
I grow too intimate
with the one addressed by the vessel
O,
the choreograph of palm
defining air,
it is her name,
the holy alphabet of lovers in a sign.

Girls in love,
I'm almost drunk.
Articulating physics I begin:
I want *Marie* to utter night for me,
to clap the music from her orphic hands,
pianist that plays the selving moon,

with fingers long and edgy,
like a star.

I fail again,
they spell intruder through the barroom smoke,
and walk away
and do not look behind.

Wait, I can explain.
I will learn to signal well.

Sappho standing on the cliff
must have gestured
large,
and loved a girl quick as dolphin
light,
and motioned as her swimmer disappeared
beyond the waves,
beyond the foam of tides.
She moved her whole body in salute;
no answer came and she despaired.
Leaving creatures of the land,
her scream was
lyric.

The dive from the cliff
is my leap now.

I enter sea:
my soundings are the dolphin sounds
calling to her friend,
wanting to follow
the liquid *Marie.*
The mouth sea-changed to snout,
but never quite.

I cannot navigate this way.
Look at me.
I chart an ocean rich in vowels.
I cannot learn your graceful play.
Tread and drift and float
are musings you must keep.

Mutes have beauties that flower
from the stalks of wrists, mimes restore

the rainforest by their shapes, where arms
like languorous vines are drooping less
than colloquy that bows and bends and snaps
beneath an argument of description.

It is so plain.
I am all thumbs
searching for that perfect synonym,
Moby Marie.

Lovers are the mutes,
and language never mars their art.
I know that now,
but I would enter Paradise disgraced,
my arms imperfect wings,
not-feather-tipped.
And I would storm the lofty clouds' domain,
defy a telepathic bliss,
to rough untold perfection with a song.
Listen.
Listen as I introduce that realm to clamor,
and let the raucous howling upstart
that you hear

let her be so fondly lettered in your brain
that you will turn to me
who touched you once in ways not understood
with dreaming verbs,
with little hands of nouns.
I loved you best with tender adjective.
And you will turn to me
and wake the ghost of angels who love sleep
surprise them from the quiet of their dream,
the voice so loud that even I will laugh
the voice so loud that even I will weep,
and turning
dare the wrath
of every mime and masque
who shamed me for my dialogue with life,
and you will turn to me and speak
and you will call my name.
Bellow from that light and noiseless place
and shout hello
and welcome dear
to shatter glass and pierce the barriers of sound.
We'll travel fast
and you will cry for loneliness like me,
admit what you denied before
and say to me,
I want the conversation back,
they never talk like you,
and I will comfort
and be a fiery pentecost of sense,
of syllables that dazzle and tell truth.

And I will whisper in your ear,
the shell I dived for long ago.

Here lovers meet across a table,
deaf mutes engaged in passionate discourse.
The heart is the genius of speech.

I translate loss.
My hands tell them a story:
the starker truth embraced by time,
for something white and distant,
gone to fathoms.

I draw them to me with a classic tale.
My right hand is a hump-backed beast,
my left a weapon in pursuit.
The language of the deaf
is cresting like a wave;
a magic dolphin churns the air,
goes speeding through a haze of smoke.
My life is rising in the ebb and flow of tide,
the dolphin on the wall is running shadow.
Two eloquent women
sign the anguish of obsession,

and the listeners,
all the listeners leave *The Tower*
to give chase.

Tonight all women lovers
board the ship of bruised desire,
tonight all women lovers
enlighten a journey under stars,
tonight all women lovers
bring the power of the secret gesture,
the centuries of Sappho with her Greek.
Tonight all lovers
and two deaf mutes in Georgia
teach my fingers
not to tear your flesh,
not to follow with the poet's clenched harpoon.

Quiet.
I am quiet now.
Silence is the waiting heart.
I form the shell with my own hands.
Place it to your ear.
A message sleeps inside a shell.
Enter the frail house of undertone.
Marie, I loved the mute.

Marie, I marveled at the mime,
and not to cry,
but speak to me.
I have been so lonely for your voice.

Scholar of Wholeness

for Rita Gabis, Regina McBride,
and Donna Masini

At sunset I grow sad the old way, balancing
my checkbook I grow sad over pieces of fading light. History
keeps sobbing childhood fractions—I grow up
in dying cities, my father's airplane drops his bombs,
one little girl is every country, when two lead
feet keep changing schools; I am the first desk in Saint Joseph's
row, Joseph is dumb to understand; in Science class the atom
splits; my brain is full of giant stairs, all shimmery
steps, I love wild numbers, winding
games; *Zero* dreams a harbor egg, and dreams
another; fear of math is fear of failure.
I am the last desk in Joseph's shrinking row, I love
whole numbers; *One* is Una, my wind-
swept shadow, as I go rushing to a doll hospital
after school, limbs of Barbara
shine in my satchel, the sidewalk
runs; *Two* draws a swan that sails off backward; my heart feels
bad with angry blood, oh do stop weeping
tiny eyes, tiny
tears and bawled-out circles; *Four* builds a nest
atop a tree, the birdmaker
cheeps; *Eight* twirls around a great
Enchanter, my father's plane is very sorry; *Nine* rolls a ball
home to the sun; I'm just a chest
of pagan babies, I carry Barbara in my sweater;
the sky prays hard: *change me, change me.* Twilight
turns: *brightly, darkly.* I remember that gold-flecked
card of the father of saints, a wondering
soul, big with vision. How truly Joseph helps a growing child!
Wrestling my angel Math, I spent three years

in the fifth grade, ashamed,
like a cold slap burning my cheek, where I refused
the sadness
fractions seemed made of . . .
Good night, sweet saint. My bones are numbered: sums of
      nebulae,
particles of trailing, magnificent dust.

The Tongues of Medusa

for Jim Moore

1

Yes!   Yes!   Yes!   Yes!

2

First I was coral:
clammy bracelet of dew;
next a hooded queen cobra

bobbing majestic.
I rattled old stones.
On the back of a diamond

I clotted red jade.
My mouth was raw cotton;
my fangs

were blue clay.
How savor strong poison?
I stored it in curls,

hiss-y with henna.
I smote and disfigured
hell or high water.

Emparadised mamba!
My head bangled copper.
Steam from a kettle

lifted me up.
I stood like a spear
on a morning of iron.

3

All creatures love height.
Upright and blazing,
I branch among flowers:

I skirr through my skin.
Weird root from the mire!
How to be murderous and survive it?

How not to end as a belt
tight around my own neck?

4

Fly with the arrow
and stalk
it
into the sharpshooting trees.
Sing up pale worms;
ensilk them
in each pierced ring of the oak.
Supper every tangled-
down serpent on beeswax.
There is this flecked bough of wisdom,
a black honeyed falling-off-thing . . .

5

Still afraid of the cure,
more afraid of the venom,

I speak for the Golden Many.

Bright flowering untree of knowledge!

I wake Eva in the wind.

6

Snake heart glitters
in the sun
long ribbon ties
braid of one
night be stormy
day be fair
she pins blossoms
in her hair
swan heart glistens
eel heart glows
now transforming
now wheel slows
proud heart glitters
in the moon
sea   hill   marsh   dune.

Psyche's Lamp

I dream you, Psyche, outside my bedroom window.
I dream you pass through screens of mesh
to find me sleeping,
and when your poignant lamp
floats
near my head,
I watch you watching me, or think
I do.
Autumn roses catch the flame.
How old is sex? I ask.
"Why I am old," you whisper kindly,
"we're a large family,
and I'm fire,
inside myself and out."
I wake to help with winter breakfast, nine
at table, I set the spoons,
and stir the cream of wheat and pulp
the grapes, this is fable
food.
Eros starts his wooden car;
disappears
into the forest.
I'm off to life.
In Troy I sack the buried moon,
and with the stars of Crete I tile the waves,
and lift my haughty face to launch fair morning,
the eyes of magnets draw me,
in sunset disarray
I shower gold, and drop
my sandal.

Sometimes I wonder who I am. History is
snowing; a starlit field
explodes in powder somewhere
close. I hold you Eros,
ocean sighs.
Petals
of hip: star-rose and merman and fiery sea.
When I swim
I drift: mouth
made of water. Eros in sperm-
light inflashes the spring.
Lightly, it is
done: mouth made
flesh. The wife of love lets down my summer hair.
The long bones of my soul
lay by the sheets. O, light
the dance! Eros
to me.
My name means music: all beautiful all night the song.

V

Thomas

Thomas, My Brother

I go to the graveyard of boats
to moan my skirled office,
this sister-wind,
from the rough bagpipes of the family.

O powerful Thomas prayer—
be in the fisherson
as in the use of high boots and decision.
Fishtails: quake alarums!
Let the tongues of brim,
ingrown and inadmissible,
hook the eternal melody.

The wharf necks into a foaming
advent of gray waves dissolving
in snow-throated edges.
The marina is empty,
though I number among the faithful
twelve splintering survivors:
these apostolic hulls
once manned silks
dry bolted up
and long saving oars
boarded in trim
woolhouses of memory,

Thomas,
as our mother
Margaret tallies the cancerous
bloodcount of her leukemia, specklike
angels are migrating faintly
in every direction
echo recalls.
For the moon-y stalks of plush are wintering well.
For the great blue heron genuflects, rises, soars.
For the mind of the marsh is a dreamless sleep long-keeping
the traveler, you.

Margaret from white blood is rocking—
the fleecey lullaby of gullah gullay cries softly her islands:
ah! all aglow our stulling cradle and lorn.
Yet old mariners in old yarns
still beg the woolly grasses
to stitch the springy motherfleet again.

Youngest:
death is the country of the argument.
I think of you speechless
amid pandemonium and flint
rubbing over and over
in the palms of your great hands
chaos and fire
for a stout-hearted woman
telling her beads.

Did the dark prince
pant for the staunch
lord of the human gesture,
plunging his fist,
his terrible quick question
into flesh godly?
was skybone fearsome?
was it granite?
Did gulls dip and descend?
wardrums of water.

Quiet one,
the patron name of your life
is the shaggy saint physical
who so loved the real
he dove with his fingers
to salvage the Christ-wreck;
stunned by a nail
he tasted platelets
of transliterate thunder.
That Thomas, *your* brother,
was a black Irish piper
with Scotch in his shoes.

Lost in the Silence of My Father

World without tongue—
    I weep and I wander
where peach trees do battle and bruiting fruit-tresses
    rupture the shank, in shear, by the season.
My mind is my spirit: before is now after.
    Numbers on clocks change hands with the Romans:
the altar of death and the white coliseum.
    I stagger to count the stains on glass soldiers
in an eerie arena malignant with cells.

    Lord, make my life from the father within me:
bless oh head, bless oh house, bless
    oh light, Saluthomas.

The Deer Man

How in the haze,
on St. Helen's island,
did Thomas entirely
conjure an elk
from a tapestry fable?
"Glaydes of Ayr, Leaping."

Peeling, gnatted,
ankle-crowned in onions,
Thomas aflame
jumps tabby seawalls.
The torch and the horn
through palm mooly meadows.

The chirr
of the towhee
clangs on a flank.
All fallow eve
amazes at Thomas!
he is first among stags.

He bolts
and he wintles
over the sandspurs
like a galleon glissando
in a loose flood of embroider;
or a drop-storm of tawny.

Tides lick and unlick
a wold moon of trouble.
Comets with tails
chase welter over.
No dream of deer—
but slayed hooves of fire.

Past famished whippets
lovesick on seaoats;
and long patrick grasses,
and leafcurls of timothy:
the deer man leaps off
the wall of a needle.

He carries his church,
a cross made of antlers,
and limps to the city,
tannic and mortal.
The deer man turned back:
but Thomas continued.

A Pearl Farmer's Almanac

By moon-snail and pince-grove
my tenants are mud-lipped.
Blue crabs are squeezing
alms to the sky.
I wake up the sundials.
I stroll with the mollusks.

The pearl of the third water
is blister-this-instant;
it whips and then hurries
the sting of a ray
grazing the surface
in a shallow of bivalves.

The pearl of the second water
is loss-under-sail;
it bores past the knurls
and knuckles of carbon.
The bark of the dogwhelk
worries grit tissue.

The pearl of the first water
is the ground-wound-of-life;
it duels and it weathers
the hurricane heart.
For a ransom of oysters
Venus opened her shell.

Pagan Hope

Take it, take it away now—
the low land, the high land,
the marsh in the middle.

I am a starred sun;
who worships a gold jig,
who runs with a fiddle.

The Mother-Daughter Face

For Gloria and Linda, who came and stood;

for mama's sisters, the soft gloves;

for the Egan clan, the Irishry and the circle big;

for five brothers, the great-shouldered men, who carried the coffin of this woman who carried them;

for my father, who saluted the earth.

Lake Lure

I wanted to be beautiful, so I read novels
by those gorse-capped Bronte sisters, who blazed a fragrant
trail—everywhere I went the unseen hovered; mysteries beyond
    me.
These were the peach-scented days when summer blossomed
out of spice-bearing orchards, out of rickety fruit stands,
out of long afternoons and flicker-dark shade—everything
I breathed was lovely; rock-trickling smoke out of the Chimney's
natural formation: shape, shadow, petal-bright-all.
I wanted to be cherished, so I washed my dusty feet in pure
spring bubbles—everywhere I went the mountain laughed.
These were the ankle-deep pastures that rang rolling bluebells;
out of small lives came cloudy humming, I moved in gnatsong.
I wanted to be beautiful, so I did nothing but wood-
walk into my own improbable glamour; mysteries around me.
This is the boathouse where I dragged my mother's stolen Camels
from the butt-pocket of my cutoffs; this is the rippling
orbit that followed the boat, oars in my hands, as I rowed
moonward and future; this is the great horned owl
that tore through my wake, three eerie elongating hoots
out of my throat, I dreamed bird-simple: all liquid
creation, all fireflies after—every story-deep
heroine mysterious inside me, and her heart soaked with heather.
Nowhere is it promised that a girl shall have a season,
but this was my summer to haunt the mountain glass of Lure.

The Unspoken

Her ambulance ride was nearly over
before she memorized the last, new word.
Nesiophile means "lover of islands."

Mama dying, where nothing solid was,
instructed us before she dove the reef.
A needle sank her vein; an ocean tore.

The cursive of her will began to print
unheard-of bruises on no word-hoard map.
Our Lady of Invention named them all.

My father drained divorce curds from his breast.
"I swore black butter couldn't melt a vow."
He kissed unconscious lips and knelt a church.

Eternity shrank her schoolbell children home;
we bawled like feelings being born.
Hourly the doctors and the nurses and

the wait—the ghastly week that made us old.
Still posted on the left side of the mirror,
vocabulary lessons for the young.

All the words are singing in the tree;
roots to the underworld—the petaled soul.
The dark sound of an uncreated mouth . . .

Atlantis disappeared inside a coma,
the surfing howl of manna filled the room,
the waves the waves the arms lapping the bed.

Phosphorescence of My Mother into the Quick of Fox Each November

I shiver in the furnace of the years.

        The chair, crushed
        in vigil flesh
        folded into a cot
        for sleeping.

        The cot was damp—
        the way pain stays
        damp on a pillow
        soaked in it.

My slip was thin.

Mama,
the night you died,
I slept like a valise,
packing of all things a chipped flask

of drawn fresh buttermilk,
until Nurse Smitty
woke my wrist.
Three on a match, and sighted.

I crossed the border into cold country.

Your breathing roughed;
tore.
My ear undreamed your mouth.
I kissed a flame.

With fingertips,
lush as fur,
I stroked your face.
Stay,

I told your cheek.

What happened happened
in my arms.
Your bay-heart quit.
My sea-work started.

War of sighs!
Isn't it finished
when the mother-daughter truce
is signed and witnessed?

My inadequate grief.

Not enough. Behind your dying
eyes I went, and went . . .
I rode the past;
I strangled hounds.

I dressed in roots. I learned one life
by heart. Fox
in my shirt: gnawed
regrets and teeth marks burning.

November has hurled the glistering foxfire

Seaward.

My Mother's Grave

Today I took the pulse of fallen leaves;
a gypsy dazzle caravan
       strums on . . .
O play, a peck of aches, stone tambourine!
As long as I keep setting this
       truth table,
a crocus feeds my mother underground.
I close my eyes, and feel her coming up.
       Delicate Spring!
Here is the town where I am always born.
Proud life that beats soft blood and pushes through.

The God-Box

It was only the marsh wearing her apron low;
it was only the channel repeating her river-name;
it was only *The Bridegroom Tree*
dropping a pomegranate
into the shade of some blood-seeded poem.

The Wand of Nature

I

The castle of my mother's beauty fires
the morning glory; lamp of stars.

How shall I tell the sadness of her leaving,
who broke a curse of mirrors on my head?

How shall I tell the pity and the shock?
I wear a funeral face to view a body.

Honey-eaters lift a white, white rose:
the living day surrenders to the dark.

II

I peer a wild, illumined image in this world.

I am a wilderness of carols.
I am the hour of larks.
I am a well of mussels, baring feet.

I am the ruddy boar that trampled shade;
     a ring of magnet eels,
     a trench of wishes.
I am the mercury of night-bruise-crossings.

III

Two sisters,
spotted with secrets,
inherit the dreamless dark. All time
is glass-walled night and rain-
drops slanting. The windows
listen: a shattering
of deer hooves and every
pane an eartip
scraping wind-green
horns. When the closet sighs
it sighs inland, folding
and unfolding mysterious froth.
By mother caught in a fastness of chain:
two small girls swam in tidal gowns.
Beauty holds them, beauty
rocks the island Fripp;
black violets sparkle the surf,
heron and fin and
old tortoise

globe. At daybreak,
Kathleen,

we shall lead our childhood shadows by the hand;
we shall praise the blue-eyed grass;
we shall swirl the toyroom dust as pearling skirts
        net oyster beds, in the silvertow of the sea;
we shall linger in the parlor of the dead;
we shall choose and discuss the matter of homesick things.

IV

Love and grief and Margaret's dresses;
this to be done,
this to be done.

The Irish call it laying down the cloth.

We say mother and begin—

the closet the latch the switch the bulk the lure the wobble
depths the sliding stalactite hangers and a scented pomander
ball of pure amber fire.

V

These nubs of season and glorious hue;
the dress of calendars and the dress of moons;
dresses pressed and cherished and hemmed and saved;
housecoats to market and suits to God;
passional scarves and stiff pilgrim collars;
the warp of bitter and wove of sweet;
dresses wooding and shelling and crabbing and sunned;
the bolt of wholeness and the sheer of parts;
hand-me-down chaff and raw joyous silk;
the dress of death-coming and the deep coffin robe;
this to be graced:
the thread of genesis, the revelation of awe;
if only we dare,
if only we dare.

VI

I believe the dignity of a child is a fragile plume.

I believe the scars of history are childhood scars
        not healed, not told, not blessed.

I believe the sibling bond is a holy trust.

I could sister you in hell, Kathleen.
I could pluck a demon's eye, and eat the sin,
I could drape the coolest snow on sunburned shoulders,
and stud such crystal flakes inside your ribs,
I could fetch a ladder tall as Eden's
light before the fall.

VII

I bring the red pear of beauty; it is good.

Her human dress, Kathleen, is us;
the delve of poetry, the dresser-of-wounds.

Antique White

In the button museum,
the dead are remembered by daughter-bright-bone.

Return

for my stepfather, John Egan

The Prodigal drives through infinite acres,
old headlamps and racing legends, overhead.
One town, one small southern town, lost in the plot.

Mind you, earth is big.

If I should find the four directions, those husky point men
     choppin' cane,
I would swim that tube of bliss that flows forever,
heading breakneck South.

Each of us has dreamed a port of call.

I can hear the creak of cool country rockers,
where velvet aunts disguise such Irish starch.
I have folded the cloth of these dwelling-place voices.

In the beginning was the land.

My people came to re-begat
the dialect of the twig.
Pilgrim debts begging to go leave.

The passage is famine, and the sky is red.

The bells of Dingle sway their solemn hips:
how shamrocks bred in fortune's ditch.
I'm not saying I understand.

This much I promise.

There will come a spring when starlight bruises sweeting yams,
and little dirt farms ride the wind,
ashes to gold.

I am a child skipping a rhyme . . .

> *Beautiful Beaufort by the sea.*
> *26 miles from Yemassee.*
> *We choose you.*

Nobody, not even a tombstone, knows my name.

Memory, my daughter, come close.
If I could baptize darkness, like a tree,
I would press a cry of herons to your heart only.

I want every homesick moon to light a crescent window.

Faraway clairvoyant families stroke the ram
until the whole feast enters my mouth.

You see, I'm here.